THE GOLDEN BOOK OF
TAORMINA

Text by
GIULIANO VALDES

BONECHI

INDEX

CASA EDITRICE BONECHI

TAORMINA
Project and editorial conception: Giampaolo Bonechi
Picture research: Serena de Leonardis
Graphic design: Laura Settesoldi
Editing: Anna Baldini

Text and collaboration
Texts: Giuliano Valdes - Editing Studio, Pisa
Text on page 91: the editors
Text on page 94: Michele Cecchi
Make-up: Studio Forma - Scarperia (Fi)
Drawings: Stefano Benini
Translation: Anthony Brierley

© Copyright   by Casa Editrice Bonechi - Firenze - Italy

The photographs belong to the Bonechi Archive and were produced by
Paolo Giambone *and* Andrea Pistolesi, *except for the following:*
pp. 6, 29, 70 below (Foto Fichera)
pp. 92, 95 (Sonia Gottardo)
pp. 54 above, 75 above, 76 below, 77, 81, 85 (Mario Tornatore)
p. 93 (Giuliano Valsecchi)

ISBN 88-8029-358-3

* * *

Detail of the scena of the Greek Theatre.

On the following page: ancient columns adorning the Greek Theatre.

INTRODUCTION AND HISTORY

*C*ommunicating with mere words the attraction of Taormina and its unique natural setting is certainly not an easy task. Consider, for a moment, that since the 18th century this enchanting little town in the province of Messina has been used as a kind of practical and experimental laboratory for what today is referred to simply as tourist promotion. Like the island of Capri - another exceptional example of order and functionality among the tourist resorts of southern Italy - Taormina rises from its pedestal, a pedestal made not of empty eulogies and declamatory rhetoric, but borne out concretely by the indescribable charm which enraptures those who for the first time contemplate this real, living landscape, however fairy-tale or dream-like it may appear. However much this idyll of the senses may resemble a painting signed by a Romantic landscape painter, the image of Taormina and its magnificent surroundings remains firm

and tangible over and beyond the painters' canvases and photographers' and film-makers' cameras, revealing the sublime essence of an unmistakable Mediterranean nature and its irresistible attraction. If in classical antiquity the terrifying vision of Mount Etna, flaming and wracked by the upheavals of the earthquake, inspired the legend of Vulcan, and the Ionian coast became the theatre of Homer's legendary characters, from Neptune, mysterious and enigmatic lord of the sea depths, to Ulysses, mariner par excellence and expression of man's hardships before the immense power of nature, to the Cyclopses (whom the stretch of coast between Aci Castello and Acireale is named after), terrifying monsters that were clearly allegories of the perils which the sea reserved for sailors, today this Mediterranean dream is within everybody's reach. There are no more monsters, either metaphysical or real. However, our approach to the town itself, its his-

3

tory, its culture, its archeological and historical treasures, its art and its splendid surroundings, should always be discreet and respectful.

Monte Tauro (397m) is the southernmost spur of the chain of the Monti Peloritani. On this limestone relief, between two deep valleys cut into the hillside by streams, a terraced plateau, shaped like an hour-glass, forms the site of Taormina. The town, surrounded by steep slopes that have been settled from the earliest times, overlooks the boundless expanse of the Ionian Sea, from the Strait of Messina and the nearby coasts of Calabria right round to the bulky, somewhat forbidding profile of Mount Etna - Vulcan's forge - a mountain perennially affected by seismic and volcanic activity. In the daytime a characteristic plume of smoke rises from the crater accompanied by a muffled rumbling sound, like the roll of distant thunder, while at night sinister flickerings and ruddy reflections light up the darkness above the mouth of the volcano.

The town of Taormina is situated 204 metres above sea level. The most pleasant approach is by a scenic road which links it with the main coast road and the motorway. The town can also be reached by a cableway, which departs from the bathing resort of Mazzarò. The beauty of the town's geographical position, the magnificent landscape with its luxuriant vegetation, one of the richest and most complete imaginable, make Taormina one of the most celebrated resorts in the Mediterranean. The historic centre, which is picturesque and unusually clean and orderly, boasts a large number of buildings and other remains from the town's Hellenistic, Roman and medieval periods, silent witnesses of an ancient past. The town is crowded throughout the year by swarms of visitors from all over the world who are attracted by the elegant shops and the welcoming atmosphere of the characteristic bars and meeting-places.

A luxuriant Mediterranean macchia covers the heights above the town, interspersed here and there with dark cypresses, the silvery-green of olive-trees, the spreading foliage of cluster pines, palm trees, cactuses and other species typical of subtropical vegetation. Orange, lemon and mandarin trees adorn the pleasant, evergreen gardens, filling the air with their intense, almost tangible Mediterranean scents. Another attraction of the town is the extremely pleasant and healthy microclimate - conditions are distinctly marine, mild and uniform with occasional wet spells. Average winter temperatures are around 11-12°C, and temperatures rarely drop below 10°C even during the harshest winters. Rainfall is very low, a characteristic of the place being the extraordinarily high number of clear, sunny days. All this, particularly since the period of the so-called 'great travellers', has made Taormina a celebrated resort, an ideal destination for holidaymakers and congressional tourists alike. There are many top-class hotels both in Taormina itself and the seaside resorts of Isola Bella, Mazzarò and Spisone. Tourists also have access to qualified, well-equipped recreational facilities capable of fulfilling the expectations of the most demanding visitor.

Taormina's exceptional geographical position, midway between Messina and Catania on the Ionian coast, makes it an ideal departure base for excursions. As well as Isola Bella, Mazzarò and Spisone, we should also mention the holiday resort of Giardini-Naxos, the Alcàntara gorge with its volcanic rock formations (the administrative border between the provinces of Messina and Catania runs along the course of the Alcàntara river), the attractive Riviera dei Ciclopi, with its picturesque fishing villages of Aci Trezza and Aci Castello, the nearby Acireale, and Mongibello (Mount Etna), the symbol of Trinacria, the original and undisputed lord of the Mediterranean volcanoes.

Characteristic festivals include the Festa del Carretto Siciliano, which takes place in May, and summer performances at the Greek Theatre. The town is also known for its flourishing craft industries - ceramics, porcelain, straw and wickerwork, textiles, lace and embroideries. We should also mention the small wooden stools, presumably of pastoral origin and extremely handy, called 'firrizzi'. Sicilian drawn-thread work, used to decorate ornamental centre cloths, tablecloths, clothes and towels, is typical of the embroideries. There are also the characteristic carved cane flutes, locally called 'friscaletti'. Marble inlay is another traditional handicraft activity. Extremely fine works, obtained with precious coloured marbles (Sicilian Yellow, Lapis lazuli, Taormina Red, Serpentine Green, Carrara Bardiglio, Pakistan Onyx and Levantine Red), are on sale at the workshop of the sculptor Gigi Samperi in Contrada Branco (Castelmola road). The traditional stroll of the cosmopolitan crowds that visit the town takes place along the central Corso Umberto, which is lined with scores of craft workshops selling a range of local products (look out for the attractive coral and volcanic stone necklaces) and tourist souvenirs. In Taormina, as in many other towns in Sicily, performances of the Teatro dei Pupi are held.

The monuments and architecture of Taormina reflect the town's millenary history: from the Greek Theatre and the Hellenistic Odeon to remains from the Roman period, like the Naumachie, a monumental nymphaeum of the imperial period. We should not forget that the most important monument in the town, the Greek Theatre, survives as an almost complete reconstruction dating from the Roman period. From the medieval period there are surviving stretches of the walls and the Castle, an invincible eagle's nest commanding a dominant position on the hillside. The medieval houses and palaces in the town, buildings of distinctive character, have a mixture of architectural styles. There is something of flamboyant Gothic in the buildings typical of the Aragonese period, while the so-called Sicilian Renaissance is markedly influenced by traces of Norman architecture, which uses pale limestone and dark volcanic pummice to create geometric ornamentation and decorative embellishments.

The first human settlements identified in Sicily date from Neolithic times. Some finds would even date the earliest presence of human beings on the island from the Paleolithic. It would seem incontrovertible, however, that the first settlements on the high rocks that are the site of present-day Taormina were made between the 13th and 12th centuries BC. Archeological investigations carried out at Cocolonazzo di Mola have probably identified traces of a Siculian necropolis. Tauromenion was therefore founded by the Siculians and very quickly established strong links with the Greeks from the city of Chalcis, who had settled along the coastal belt and founded the colony of Naxos. Naxos was destroyed by Dionysius, the tyrant of Syracuse, in 392 BC. In 358 BC the survivors of Naxos, who had reformed under Andromachus, father of the Greek historian Timaeus, established the first nucleus of the Greek city at Tauromenion. Under the enlightened

An impressive aerial view of Taormina.

government of Agathocles the new city was reorganized administratively, was given a new constitution and resisted the repeated attempts of the Carthaginians to subdue it. For long conditioned by the fortunes of the nearby Syracuse, it was taken by Agathocles, tyrant of Syracuse, whose aim was to extend Greek hegemony all over the island. The Carthaginians, intoleratant of his expansionist tendencies, defeated Agathocles at Ecnomo in 310 BC, near present-day Poggio Sant'Angelo, after already having had effective control of Tauromenion for five years. Later the city passed into the hands of Tyndarion, who opened the way for Pyrrhus to oppose the Carthaginians. Taken by the Syracusan Hieron II, the ally of the Carthaginians in the first Punic War against Rome, it was brought under Roman control only after the death of the tyrant of Syracuse. Renamed Tauromenium, because of its strategic importance and its loyal alliance with Rome, it was given the status of 'civitas foederata', enjoying particular immunities and fiscal privileges that had few equals in the Sicily of the time. At the time of the Servile War Tauromenium acted like a catalyst for the rebelling slaves until Rupilius quashed the revolt in 132 BC. In 34 BC Octavian founded a colony here, appreciating the strategic importance of the site. Under the long-lasting period of Roman rule the whole of Sicily, though Taormina in particular, was the recipient of a large number of public works, and an increasingly extensive road network was laid out. Due to its highly agreeable position

and its splendid Mediterranean climate, wealthy Roman patricians preferred Taormina, like Capri, for their magnificent residences. Indeed, the construction of luxurious villas and sumptuous houses is borne out by the finds of fragments of marble pavements among the numerous archeological remains. With the fall of the Roman Empire the town followed the fortunes of the Byzantines in Sicily, and towards the end of the 9th century it had become the main centre of the island's Byzantine dominions. From the first half of the 9th century Sicily was beset by Saracen raids. Taormina, which had already had a foretaste of the new threat in 902, was besieged by Ibn Ahmed and after surrendering was razed to its foundations in 962. Rebuilt as Almuzia, from the name of the caliph Al Muizz who had fallen in love with Taormina's beauty, it was conquered by the armed forces of the Norman leader Roger de Hautville, who had laid siege to the town and stormed it in 1079. The arrival of the Normans signalled the expulsion of the Saracens from the island. Controlled by Messina, which undermined the town's independence, Taormina was sacked during the insurrections of 1168 and 1261. At the time of the rebellion known as the Sicilian Vespers (1282) Taormina sided with the Aragonese. During the civil war it was the object of a dispute between the Chiaramonte family and the crown. In 1410, in Palazzo Corvaia, the Sicilian parliament assembled and proclaimed Federico di Luna king of Sicily. Later the town was the object of trade and exchange on

View of Taormina with Mount Etna in the background.

the part of the Spanish monarchy, to which it always manifested its loyalty, even at the time of the Messina uprising of 1675. Occupied by the soldiers of Louis XIV of France, it was soon given back its freedom. Taken by Philip V of Spain, it was defended by Filangieri, who was awarded the title of Duke of Taormina. The town, called Tavormina *in the Bourbon period, generously participated in the struggle against the Bourbons, lords of the two Sicilies. On 9 April 1860 it escaped from their control for a short period and was finally freed of it immediately after on the occasion of Garibaldi's historic achievement (May-July 1860) which would see Sicily united with the nascent Italian state.*
The history of tourism in Taormina began in the 18th century, although the pleasantness of its geographical position and the beauty of the Mediterranean setting had of course exerted an irresistible appeal ever since the Roman period. Artists, painters, photographers, writers, poets and intellectuals, scholars of various disciplines and 'great travellers' have contributed to the present fortune of this little corner of paradise in eastern Sicily. The first admirers of classical Taormina, of the Hellenistic remains and its Theatre, were the Dutch scholar J. Philipp d'Orville, in 1727, and the German Hermann von Riedesel, in 1767. In the last quarter of the century the town was visited by the German landscape painter J. Philipp Hackert, who painted the View of Etna from Taormina *(1777). The list of illustrious travellers 'en-*

chanted' by Taormina includes the French geologist Dolomieu, with his fellow countrymen Denon, Despres and Houel, and the Englishmen Brydone, Hamilton, Knight and Swinburne. Goethe, Guy de Maupassant, Edward Lear and others arrived later. The real 'discovery' of Taormina is traditionally associated with the German aristocrat O. von Geleng (1863), the author of ecstatic paintings. The photographs of Bridges, Piot, Sommer, Conrad and Rive followed, but it was above all W. von Gloeden, who moved here in 1875 to complete his thesis, who in his celebrated photographic portraits of the Ephebi of Taormina *conveyed a classical, sensual and decadent image. Taormina's fame was now at its peak. Among its residents and visitors were Thomas Mann, Somerset Maugham, André Gide and Florence Trevelyan, the latter being responsible for the building of the bizarre* Victorian Follies. *Other famous people who have lived here in the 20th century include Gabriele d'Annunzio, Anatole France, Edward VII and George V of England, Wilhelm II of Germany and representatives of various illustrious families (Rothschild, Krupp, Morgan), as well as the transalpine writer R. Peyrefitte. Alongside these famous names there is always touristic Taormina, always ready to open its arms to you and sweep you away forever with the help of a fiery red sunset over the waters of the Ionian Sea amid the palm trees and the scent of orange blossom, while in the background the great volcano reminds us that this is still the land of myth and legend.*

1 Porta Catania
2 Palazzo dei Duchi di Santo Stefano
3 Church of the Carmine
4 Cathedral of San Nicolò
5 Piazza Fountain
6 San Domenico
7 Badia Vecchia
8 Church of the Visitation
9 Torre dell'Orologio
10 Church of San Giuseppe
11 Church of Sant'Agostino
12 Piazza IX Aprile
13 Odeon
14 Church of Santa Caterina
   d'Alessandria
15 Palazzo Corvaja
16 Church of the Cappuccini
17 Church of San Pancrazio
18 Greek Theatre
19 Gardens of the Villa Comunale Duca
   Colonna Di Cesarò
20 Sanctuary of Madonna della Rocca

A picturesque view of Corso Umberto where it joins Piazza IX Aprile.

Piazza IX Aprile, with the Torre dell'Orologio, the Church of San Giuseppe, whose bell-tower and spire are visible, and the imposing Sanctuary of the Madonna della Rocca high in the background.

PIAZZA IX APRILE

The square opens out of the central street, *Corso Umberto,* breaking the continuity of the town's central axis which runs from Porta Catania to Porta Messina. Because of its 'strategic' position the piazza is the main focus of social gathering in the Ionian town. It has characteristics similar to those of other high open spaces, being a unique, attractive and unrivalled observation point. Looking out over the iron balustrade surrounding the square, we can admire the unmistakable profile of Mount Etna, snow-capped until well into the season, often smoking and illuminated by fiery flashes of fire at night, a veritable sentinel of Ionian Sicily as well as a natural beacon for navigators. The volcano blends with the natural and the humanized landscape, an inseparable dual concept in the most typical iconography of this land. "Mount Etna from Taormina is a huge chimney or an enormous column", wrote the geographer A. F. Busching in descriptive vein. Looking now towards the Ionian coast, we see the picturesque, crescent-shaped bay of Giardini-Naxos, situated between Capo Taormina and Capo Schisò. Concluding this panoramic observation is Capo Taormina, the extreme spur of the hill on which the Greek Theatre stands. The piazza, shaded and embellished by plants, which in spring burst into glorious colour, is the usual destination of the walks of tourists and visitors, the compulsory stop of the evening promenade along the Corso. Elegant open-air bars and meeting-places invite one to take a pleasant rest, perhaps sip a characteristic 'granita' of coffee with cream, or yield to some choice titbit, like Sicilian 'cassata' or melon jelly. From on high the mighty bastions of the Castle survey the teeming cosmopolitan crowd below.

Two views of Piazza IX Aprile with its most characteristic landmarks.

The old Torre dell'Orologio along Corso Umberto.

TORRE DELL'OROLOGIO

Piazza IX Aprile is not only a scenic observation point, a charming 'salon' or a continental tea of the mad hatter where you wonder who will end up in the teapot (paraphrasing what the English writer D. H. Lawrence noted in a letter to a friend). It is surrounded and ennobled by buildings of considerable monumental and architectural interest. The Torre dell'Orologio, or Clock Tower, dominates the lower side of the square and actually straddles the central *Corso Umberto*. The building, also called the **Porta di Mezzo**, forms an entrance leading into the medieval town, separating the latter from classical and Hellenistic Taormina. The stone structure is surmounted by a crenellated battlement and a clock is set into the upper part of the facade. The gateway consists of an elegant arch in blocks of dressed stone. The tower was built in the Middle Ages over an earlier foundation of Hellenistic walls. The building was restored in the second half of the 17th century because the original structure had been damaged.

CHURCH OF SAN GIUSEPPE

Another important piece in the unique mosaic of the urban fabric of *Piazza IX Aprile* is the church of S. Giuseppe (late 17th C.), which occupies the lower portion of its western side. The building is approached by a double flight of steps. The Baroque **facade** has a middle portion enclosed by two pilaster strips. The main door is flanked by two columns and surmounted by a Baroque tympanum, and there are three windows, the larger central one containing a large statue. The outer parts of the facade are set off by the undulating line of the roof, crowned by pinnacles and statues. At the side rises the elegant **campanile**, whose cusp is reminiscent of Aragonese architectural styles. The **interior**, a single large hall with a triumphal arch, is lavishly decorated with 18th-century stuccoes. Various 17th-century canvases illustrate *Episodes from the Life of the Virgin*.

The Baroque facade of the Church of San Giuseppe.

The Church of San Giuseppe, detail of one of the external flights of steps and a view of the Baroque interior.

The bare facade of the Church of Sant'Agostino and a detail
of its interior, now used as the town library.

Piazza IX Aprile with the Church of Sant'Agostino and a
detail of the Gothic ornamentation of its facade.

CHURCH OF SANT'AGOSTINO

The church, dedicated to the bishop of Hippo, was in the
past consecrated to the cult of St Sebastian. It closes the
northern side of *Piazza IX Aprile*. This building, originally Gothic, was built in the second half of the 15th century. The rather bare **facade** is set off by the Gothic arched
door and by a splendid rose-window, while the **campanile** at the side is distinguished by its belfry with small
Gothic arches and cornices in volcanic stone. The secu-
larized interior now houses the town library.

A picturesque view of Corso Umberto and one of its distinctive religious motifs of clear Byzantine inspiration.

Picturesque view of the centre of Taormina, immersed in palm-trees and lush vegetation.

Two other views of Corso Umberto.

CORSO UMBERTO

The high street of Taormina is named after Umberto I, son of Victor Emmanuel II. It describes a semicircle in the urban fabric of the old city and links **Porta Catania** in the south with **Porta Messina** in the north. Much of it is typically medieval in appearance. The street is narrow and devoid of pavements and is lined with buildings, many of which are obviously very old. Numerous doorways are typical of the architecture of the 15th century, having splendid Gothic forms. Many lanes and alleys lead off it, many of which are spanned by arches. These give picturesque glimpses of the surrounding hillsides with their luxuriant vegetation, gardens and villas, and the maze of medieval alleys below against the background of the blue sea. Occasional small squares with bars and meeting-places and a great variety of elegant shop-windows make a walk along the street a highly agreeable experience.

From a vantage-point on Monte Tauro a view of the town of Taormina below and the deep blue waters of the Ionian Sea beyond.

The distinctive facade of the Cathedral of San Nicolò and a Fountain with mythological decoration in the foreground.

CATHEDRAL OF SAN NICOLÒ

Taormina's *Piazza del Duomo* is situated in the southern area of the town, the more obviously medieval and Renaissance part. Looking onto it is the **Palazzo Municipale**, which has 17th-century architectural elements. The outstanding building of this open space is the cathedral, named after *San Nicolò*, in front of which is an elegant fountain. At first sight the building, with its basilical structure, looks more like a fortress than a church, an impression heightened by the fact that it is made entirely of rough stone blocks and crowned by a crenellated battlement along its entire perimeter. The building dates from the 13th century and was built on the site of an earlier religious building. It was rebuilt between the 15th and 16th centuries and again rebuilt in the 18th century. The rough **facade** is embellished by a fairly elaborate 16th-century rose-window and by two Gothic-arched windows. The main door, dating from the 17th century, is Mannerist in inspiration. It is crowned by a tympanum supported by fluted columns and bears an intricate decorative motif, both in the architrave and columns. There

are two fine portals in the **side walls** of the cathedral: the one on the left is 15th century and has superb ornamentation with a representation of *Saints Peter and Paul with the Blessing Christ* in the architrave; the right-hand portal is 16th century. The **interior** conforms to the usual basilical scheme, being divided into a nave and two side aisles by huge granite columns, which, according to a tradition, may have been taken from the Greek Theatre. Some interesting works of art grace the interior decoration of the church: note the 16th-century polyptych by Antonello De Saliba (*Virgin and Child with Saints Jerome and Sebastian; The Dead Christ with Saints Lucy and Agatha; Christ with the Apostles*); a painting by Antonino Giuffré (*Visitation with Saints Joseph and Zacharias, 15th C.*); a *Madonna and Child*, a fine 16th-century sculpture in alabaster of the Gaginesque circle; a statue of *St Agatha* (M. Montanini) of the same period, and a *Madonna and Child Enthroned with Saints John the Baptist and James, God the Father and the Crucifix*, a 16th-century painting by A. Franco.

The Cathedral of San Nicolò: these pictures show the ornate main portal of the church and some details of its intricate decoration.

The Cathedral of San Nicolò: some views of the interior with the baptismal font and the polyptych on wood by Antonello De Saliba (16th century).

On the following pages, two celebrated pictorial works in the Cathedral of San Nicolò: the polyptych on wood by Antonello De Saliba ('Virgin and Child with Saints Jerome and Sebastian', 'The Dead Christ with Saints Lucy and Agatha' - 1504); the painting by Antonino Giuffré ('Visitation with Saints Joseph and Zacharias' - 1463).

PIAZZA FOUNTAIN

The Fountain adorning Taormina's *Piazza del Duomo* is a particularly fine element in the town's urban decoration. It was made in 1635 in the Baroque style. The base, with its slightly elliptical plan, is formed by a short flight of steps. At the tips of the ellipse are four smaller fountains, each formed by a short cylindrical shaft supporting a circular basin. On top of each shaft is a *sea horse*, a clear mythological allegory that reappears in the central body of the fountain. The latter consists of two basins one on top of the other, supported and populated by figures drawn from mythology. Observe the fine workmanship of the sculptures. The crowning decoration of the Fountain consists of what has become the symbol of the town: a *two-legged female centaur*. The mythological figure wears a crown and is holding a globe in its left hand.

A detail of the Fountain in Piazza del Duomo with the cathedral in the background.

A detail of the Fountain of Piazza del Duomo: the two-legged female centaur standing as a symbol of the town.

A nocturnal view of the Fountain with the Cathedral of San Nicolò; a detail (sea-horse) of the decoration of the Fountain.

A splendid aerial view of Taormina with the complex of San Domenico and the coast of Giardini-Naxos in the background.

San Domenico, with its cloisters, seen from above; today it is a luxury hotel.

San Domenico, an interior room and a view of the cloister.

On the following pages: San Domenico various glimpses of the splendid gardens of the premises and various other images of this elegant hotel complex.

SAN DOMENICO

The complex of San Domenico, an inseparable part of the town's history, culture and tourism, is situated on the south-eastern spur of the terrace of Taormina. It occupies a commanding position with good views in magnificent natural surroundings. Visible from its beautifully kept gardens and windows is "a landscape in which there is everything that seems created on Earth to seduce the eyes, the mind and the imagination", as the 19th-century French writer Guy de Maupassant remarked joyfully when referring to Taormina. What today is the *Grand Hotel San Domenico Palace,* that is, a top-class hotel which has preserved some elements of the original monastic furnishings and decoration, was, until 1866, a large religious complex. San Domenico was built in the second half of the 14th century on the wishes of a local nobleman, Fra Girolamo de Luna. Later, Damiano Rosso degli Altavilla, prince of Cerami, who in turn had taken up the religious orders, left all his property and possessions to the monastery. In his

will he stipulated that his properties were to be returned to the family if they had a use that was not religious. In 1866 a law of Pasquale Stanislao Mancini revoked the agreement with the Holy See, the religious orders were abolished and their possessions expropriated. The complex of buildings comprising San Domenico thus returned to the princes of Cerami, who decided to convert it into a prestigious hotel residence. Of the old group of buildings the original monastery has survived, including the splendid **cloister** of the 16th century and other equally charming minor cloisters. Of the original church, formerly dedicated to *Saint Agatha* and later to *Saint Mary of the Annunciation*, only the **bell-tower** has survived (17th-18th century), the rest having been destroyed during the bombing of 1943. The superb garden, situated at the back of the complex, is stunning for the variety of plants and flowers it contains, in the flowering season a compendium of one of the most beautiful landscapes in the Mediterranean.

Corso Umberto and other typical views of the charming streets of Taormina. The lush vegetation and rare plant species typical of hot climates, in wonderful harmony with a 'solar', Mediterranean architecture, are vivid, characterful images which attract the attention of tourists and enrich the humanized landscape of this pearl of the Ionian coast.

PALAZZO CORVAJA

The palace is one of the most representative buildings in Taormina, not only because of its original architecture and its historical importance, but also because it cannot be avoided by those who visit the Greek Theatre. The first fabrication of this building dates from the Arab period (11th century), when it consisted of a tower-like edifice, possibly part of a fortified construction. Between the 14th and 15th centuries the other parts of the palace were added. Today we see not only the ancient Arabic core, but the later Norman, Gothic, Catalan and Chiaramontane elements. In 1410 the Sicilian parliament assembled here and elected Federico di Luna king of Sicily. The building is crowned by crenellations of various manufacture. Note the elegant mullioned windows of Catalan style adorning the right wing of the palace, where there is also a superb three-light window on the same side as the main door, it too extremely elaborate. In the splendid courtyard is a balcony with sculpted panels portraying the *Creation of Eve*, *Original Sin* and the *Expulsion from Paradise*. An inscription above the stairs mentions that this was the favourite refuge of its owner: *Esto. Michii. Locv. Refvgii.* Various Latin epigraphs on the building's facade celebrate Prudence, Justice, Temperance and Fortitude.

A view of Palazzo Corvaja.

View of Palazzo Corvaja and the Church of Santa Caterina d'Alessandria.

Palazzo Corvaja, detail of a mullioned window, with the cornice decorating the facade, and the delightful inner courtyard.

CHURCH OF SANTA CATERINA D'ALESSANDRIA

The church stands next to Palazzo Corvaja and dates from the 17th-18th century. The **facade**, above which is a short bell-tower, is simple and adorned with an 18th-century Baroque door. Above it, inside a niche, is a sculptured likeness of *St Catherine of Alexandria* executed in the 18th century by P. Greco. The **interior**, of modest proportions, is brightly lit and characterized by the usual Baroque ornamentation. At the high altar, but also at the side ones, are fine spiral columns. Among the works of art there is a marble statue of *St Catherine of Alexandria* (late 15th C.), a *Martryrdom of St Catherine* (high altar, J. Vignerio, 16th C.), a *Triumph of the Cross* (17th C.) and a *Glory of the Madonna with Carmelite Saints* of the same period, and a wooden *Crucifix* (18th C.). The distinctive feature of the building is its foundations, which are laid over the remains of a Hellenistic temple and easily visible from inside the church.

Church of Santa Caterina d'Alessandria: a view of the luminous Baroque interior; a detail of the foundations, built over a Hellenistic temple.

Facade of the Church of Santa Caterina d'Alessandria with details (below) of the main and side portails.

NAUMACHIE

These extensive remains of the Roman period are among the most representative in the whole of Sicily. They consist of a long brick wall dating from the Imperial age, which was restored only in 1943. The restoration also brought to light part of the original pavement. Although these Roman remains, running parallel to the upper stretch of *Corso Umberto*, are aesthetically diminished by the row of houses built above them, the monumental row of the 18 larger niches is nonetheless remarkable. These are alternated with smaller rectangular niches. The entire facade is 122 metres long and 5 metres high. Theories about its original use vary: it may have been a monumental nymphaeum; it certainly was not used for the representation of naval battles (despite the fact that the name suggests the contrary); much more probably it was a *gymnasium* or a place for gymnastic exercises.

View of the Naumachie, a remarkable example of the town's Roman architecture.

A detail of the cavea and a view of the Odeon.

On the following pages: Taormina and the sea seen from the rugged limestone slopes of Monte Tauro.

ODEON

The Small Theatre, a name which distinguishes it from the well-known Greek Theatre, is a building dating from the Imperial age (2nd C. AD) which originally must have had a roof. For many centuries hidden by the proliferation of other buildings, it was finally excavated in 1893. The auditorium, made of brick, is divided into five segments. Access to the stairs, from the lower part, was gained by means of a covered corridor, while the upper part of the space used by the public could be reached by way of the vomitories, which were served by a corridor that surrounded the whole structure. The stage of the Odeon, along the longer side, was made from a Hellenistic temple (the divinity to which it was dedicated being unknown), the same temple whose remains can be seen in the substructures of the church of Santa Caterina d'Alessandria. We know for certain that it was a Doric temple whose naos was surrounded by columns. At the side of the stage are traces of a room reserved for the actors.

Two views of the splendid Greek Theatre situated on the rocky promontory overlooking the sea, and two images of the entrance to the Theatre.

GREEK THEATRE

The image of Taormina's Greek Theatre, a marvel of the human mind embodying art and history, landscape and nature, culture and enchanted myth, continues to evoke the idealizing spirit and hedonistic intent of its designers and builders more than 2000 years after they lived. The ruins of this excellently preserved ancient monument, which has in large part been restored to the splendour it must have had originally, speak to us of the greatness of a people, of its civilization and of its achievements. They also tell us of a profound respect for the importance of beauty, of a love for theatre, drama, tragedy and stage representation; they tell of the characters and authors, poets and philosophers, thinkers and sculptors who sublimated the myth of Helladic civilization well beyond its native shores, along the coasts of the Mediterranean, in the most distant corners of Magna Grecia. In our own time, it is worth recalling that this masterpiece of the ancient city, which commands a magnificent view over the

clear blue waters of the Ionian Sea, the snow-capped smoking mountain and the surrounding hills and citrus groves, has become the image of tourism in Sicily *par excellence*. For almost three hundred years the Theatre of Taormina, with the help of its unique setting, has become a kind of logo for the entire island. Situated in the inner part of the limestone promontory which extends towards Capo Taormina, and dominating the glorious coast between the latter, Isola Bella, Capo Sant'Andrea, Mazzarò and Lido Spisone, the Greek Theatre lies outside the urbanized fabric of the town. Various epigraphic references allow us to date this construction to the Hellenistic period, to the period of the tyrant Hieron II (3rd C. BC). In order to realize this immense building project the summit of the natural saddle on which the theatre now stands needed to be levelled. It has been estimated that no less than 100,000 cubic metres of limestone rock were removed from the site. The Theatre of Taormina is the

Greek Theatre, a detail of the scena and a view from the cavea towards the town and Monte Tauro.

On the following pages:
Greek Theatre, snow-capped Etna framing the ancient remains and their magnificent surroundings; reconstruction of the ancient Greek Theatre.

largest in Sicily after that of Syracuse (109m in diameter; orchestra 35m across), its majestic and imposing monumentality making it one of the most eminent and important examples of theatre building of the Hellenistic and Roman periods. From the 2nd C. AD, at the height of the Imperial age, the Romans radically modified the building, the aim being to adapt the structure according to the Roman idea of the amphitheatre and to satisfy the Roman taste for spectacle entertainment. Originally conceived as a place for the staging of plays or for musical performances, the Theatre gave way to gladiatorial contests (*gladiatores*), naval battles (*naumachiae*) and hunting spectacles (*venationes*). This involved an extension of the orchestra, which as a result became an arena, and the construction of a high podium to protect the spectators from the risks involved in certain types of spectacle; trenches were dug for the fights between gladiators and between gladiators and wild animals. The capacious cavea, entirely hewn out of the limestone rock, could accommodate up to 5,400 spectators. Today it is still divided into nine wedge-sheped segments served by eight flights of steps. In the central sections some old blocks have been repositioned, thus partially reconstructing the original tiered seating. In the medieval period the Theatre was used as a kind of quarry for materials to erect palaces and embellish churches. According to one tradition, the columns of the cathedral were removed from the scena. In the Roman period, the cavea was surrounded by two arcades; the upper one was supported by columns; below, in the space between the columns, were niches containing statues. The backstage, facing the city, had a distinctly monumental appearance, being embellished with friezes,

fresco paintings and sculptures. Behind the scena, a columned portico accommodated the spectators during intervals in performances. The *parascenia,* or places reserved for the actors and for storing stage scenery, have survived in part. Of the double row of columns, which once adorned the stage, only a few elements remain. They were erected in the course of a heavy-handed restoration carried out in the last century. Today, in the restored and re-adapted stage structure, known universally for the perfection of its acoustics, plays and other stage performances are held during the summer months. Also worth a mention are the remains of a small **Temple**, situ-

Greek Theatre, a view of the cavea and a detail of the ancient tiers of seats.

Greek Theatre, two views of the scena.

These photographs show just how intact the ancient Greco-Roman ruins are. The works in brick, the arches, the columns and what remains of the colonnades exist in a close symbiosis with a hardy, exuberant vegetation. The silence of the ruins, interrupted only by the whispering of the wind, the Mediterranean scents, the light and the colours make this place intensely majestic and evocative.

Greek Theatre, details of the walls.

Greek Theatre, view from the Theatre over Taormina and towards Mount Etna.

ated above the eastern part of the cavea, and the **Antiquarium**, which displays important finds discovered during the excavations. Among these are a Roman sarcophagus with *Dionysian scenes*, various tablets bearing the reports of the city magistrates from the 2nd C. BC to the Imperial age, Greek epigraphs and a headless Hellenistic torso representing *Dionysus* or *Apollo*. From the top of the steps of the Theatre is a unique and unrepeatable view, dominated by Mount Etna, "the nearest thing to the contemplation of Eden", as Cardinal J. Henry Newman wrote in 1833.

VILLA COMUNALE
DUCA COLONNA DI CESARÒ

Taormina's public gardens flank the *Via Bagnoli Croce* and form one of the most delightful places in the town. It is truly a green haven, populated by an amazing and composite variety of plant species. The lush vegetation, palms, cactuses and flowers, whose blooms set this Ionian Eden ablaze with colour, offer refreshing shade and spectacle even in the hottest weather. The rarefied sea air and balmy fragrances are a rare and effective cure-all, while here and there are breathtakingly scenic views. Also worth a mention are the **Victorian Follies**, a series of ornamental toy-buildings which Florence Trevelyan had built at the end of the 19th century.

The so-called Victorian Follies are situated in the luxuriant gardens of the Villa Comunale Duca Colonna di Cesarò.

A delightful avenue of the Villa Comunale.

From the Villa Comunale a view of the town of Taormina dominated by the Castle and by the Sanctuary of the Madonna della Rocca.

View of the Victorian Follies, decorative
architecture of the Villa Comunale.

These photographs show other views of the Villa Comunale,
with its splendid decoration of flowers and plants and 'toy
constructions'.

Gothic and Norman motifs in the elegant facade of
Palazzo dei Duchi di Santo Stefano.

The elegant Palazzo dei Duchi di Santo Stefano
overlooking a delightful courtyard.

PALAZZO DEI DUCHI DI SANTO STEFANO

This palace, one of the best preserved examples of
Norman architecture in Taormina, stands in the immedi-
ate vicinity of Porta Catania. Its construction dates from
the second half of the 13th century and the beginning of
the 14th century. The building has incorporated various
earlier wall structures which probably date from the period of Arab rule. This palace was the residence of the
dukes of Santo Stefano of Spain; it also housed the De
Spuches family, who were made princes of Galati. The
best overall view of this splendid building can be obtained from the small but very attractive garden, with its
pretty plants and palm trees. The recent restoration, made
necessary after the heavy damage suffered in the Second
World War, has returned the palace to its former splendour. It is not difficult to recognize the salient features of
the architecture of the Sicilian Middle Ages, represented
here in a mixture of styles, from Gothic and Norman to
Catalan, Arabic and Chiaramontane. The building, built

entirely of stone, still has huge blocks of dressed stone in
its lower part. Further up, on the first floor, is an elegant
line of simple mullioned windows. A projecting string-
course separates the first floor from the second, where
there is another row of mullioned windows. The latter are
of even finer manufacture when compared to those of the
first floor, having gracious trilobate arches at the top of
the window and a rose-window containing a six-pointed
star of excellent workmanship. But the real peculiarity of
the building, which has the features of a tower more than
those of a palace, is the elegant bichrome cornice which
surrounds the roof: a series of three-lobed arches supports
a spectacular mosaic of alternating white limestone and
dark volcanic stone. At the top is an incomplete series of
Ghibelline crenellations. The interior is used by the *G.
Mazzullo Foundation*. The graphic works and sculptures
of this artist are displayed in the garden and on the three
floors of the palace.

A picturesque view of the Badia Vecchia, framed by the imposing outline of Mount Etna.

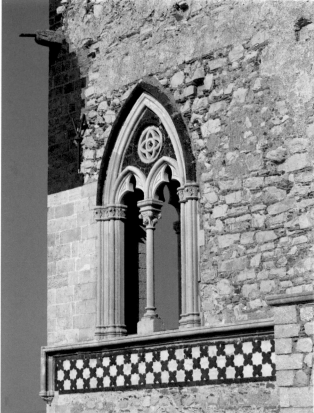

Badia Vecchia, a splendid combination of various types of stone embellishes the facade of the 'Badiazza'.

BADIA VECCHIA

This tower of the Norman period is also known as the *Badiazza*, a popular name which evidently refers to its early use as a monastery. The present building is probably the surviving part of what at some time must have been a larger complex. Because of its fortress-like appearance, the preciousness of its ornamentation, but above all because of its extremely pleasant setting high up on the hill, dominating the medieval part of the town, it is one of the most representative buildings in Taormina. The Badia Vecchia was restored, with elaborate ornamentation in the 14th century. Note the splendid cornice separating the first from the second floor; here too, as in the Palazzo dei Duchi di Santo Stefano, there is ample use of polychrome intarsia, obtained with the use of stones of different colours. The handsome crowning of Ghibelline crenellations, the various styles of splendid mullioned windows, and the outer staircase confer further elegance to the old building.

The facade of the Church of San Pancrazio and its bell-tower; the little piazza, with the airy arcaded precinct in front of the building, is shaded by palm trees.

CHURCH OF SAN PANCRAZIO

The church, its facade surrounded by an airy portico shaded by palms, is in *Largo Giove Serapide*, just beyond Porta Messina. The building was built on what remains of an ancient temple consecrated to the cult of Jove Serapis. As in the church of Santa Caterina d'Alessandria, here too parts of the building lie over the foundations of the ancient Hellenistic city. The facade is distinguished by its Baroque **portal**, which is reached by a short flight of steps. At the sides are two statues, one of *St Pancras* (left) and the other of St *Procopius* (right), each flanked by two columns. The church **interior** has paintings of the 18th century. The entire building, built in the late 17th century, has Baroque features which are also present at the top of the **campanile**.

NECROPOLIS

Just outside the town, in a wooded area along the *Via Luigi Pirandello*, is a stretch of ancient wall with rows of recesses symmetrically arranged one above the other. These are not Roman ruins, as we might too hastily imagine, but the remains of an old Byzantine cemetery, probably used again in the Arab period.

CHURCH OF SANTI PIETRO E PAOLO

The church is situated outside the town, not far from the Necropolis, on the *Via Luigi Pirandello*, which links Taormina with the coast (SS. 144). The old stone apsidiole reveals the ancient origins of the first church, which was presumably built in the Byzantine period over the remains of a Hellenistic temple. Discoveries by archeologists have confirmed the antiquity of this site. The present church is datable to the 15th century. The **facade** is of the 18th century, while the **interior**, with its division into nave and side aisles, has elements which are more Gothic in style.

A detail of the necropolis with its burial niches; a view of the Church of Santi Pietro e Paolo.

SANCTUARY OF MADONNA DELLA ROCCA

The panoramic Sanctuary, a religious complex partly hewn out of the bare rock, stands on a limestone spur on the south-eastern slopes of Monte Tauro. It is marked by a white Cross clearly visible even from Taormina, and can be reached by turning off the *Rotabile Castelmola*. Linked to the cult of the Madonna, the Sanctuary is the destination of pilgrimages on 20 September, when its feast-day is celebrated. From the terrace in front of the facade is a magnificent view of Taormina, the Ionian coast and the grandiose natural backdrop of Mount Etna.

The Sanctuary of Madonna della Rocca dominating the complex of San Domenico and the seaside resort of Giardini-Naxos.

View from Monte Tauro with the Sanctuary of Madonna della Rocca, part of the town of Taormina and the Ionian coast.

The rugged, precipitous limestone slopes of Monte Tauro, seen from the town, crowned by the sanctuary dedicated to Mary, the object of devoted pilgrimages; a detail of the Sanctuary of Madonna della Rocca.

Castelmola, two views of the picturesque settlement situated on a panoramic rock.

CASTELMOLA

Although situated at only 529m above sea level, this very ancient settlement has all the characteristics of a veritable eagle's nest. Because of its position on the summit of an inaccessible limestone outcrop, it has always been Taormina's protective bastion against insidious threats from inland. A Siculian necropolis at Cocolonazzo attests to the antiquity of the settlement, which some have identified as ancient *Mylai*. Razed to the ground by Dionysius in the first half of the 4th century, it was quickly rebuilt. In 902, during the period of Arab rule, it was destroyed again. From *Piazza Sant'Antonio*, with a good view of the medieval Castle below, Taormina and the Ionian riviera framed by the smoking profile of Mount Etna, we climb to the **Castle**, or more precisely what remains of a 16th-century fortress. Other important sites in the village, with its narrow streets lined with characteristic craft workshops and souvenir shops, are the 17th-century **Church of San Giorgio**, the 16th-century **Parish Church** of the 16th century and the **Caffè San Giorgio**, which has become a must for both illustrious visitors and simple enthusiasts of this fascinating corner of Ionian Sicily.

MEDIEVAL CASTLE

The imposing remains of a medieval fortification are clearly visible from Taormina on the top of Monte Tauro (397m). Also called *Castel Taormina*, it occupies the site where it is believed the ancient acropolis of the Hellenistic city stood. Its attractive position and superb setting make it a compulsory visit for those who wish to be fully acquainted with Taormina. The interesting remains are reached by a flight of steps that departs from the Sanctuary of Madonna della Rocca. An alternative is the mule track that branches off the *Via Circonvallazione*, not far from *Largo Giove Serapide*. The remains of this stronghold consist of the imposing keep, the walls surmounted by a tower, a cistern and an underground tunnel. The castle dominates the steep, cactus-studded slopes of Monte Tauro overlooking the enchanting Mediterranean coast.

A Gothic arch built into the walls; the walls of the medieval Castle on Monte Tauro.

Partial view of the town looking towards Capo Taormina.

View of Capo Taormina jutting into the deep blue waters of the Ionian Sea.

CAPO TAORMINA

There is a common thread linking the coasts in the vicinity of Taormina, as if they had been shaped by a single hand to convey the enchanting beauty of one of the most picturesque and evocative landscapes in eastern Sicily. Capo Taormina forms the southernmost spur of the Monti Peloritani chain, which through Montagna Grande (1374m), Monte Veneretta (884m) and Monte Tauro (397m) extends as far as the sea. It marks the northern limit of the gulf formed by Capo Taormina and Capo Schisò, in the centre of which lies the holiday resort of Giardini-Naxos, famous for its archeological remains. To the north of Capo Taormina, and between it and Capo Sant'Andrea, is the idyllic Baia delle Sirene. Never was a name more appropriate for exalting the appeal of this picturesque inlet, framed by the blue Ionian waters, the rich green of the Mediterranean macchia which cloaks the rugged limestone cliffs that drop sheer into the sea, and the spectacular group of rocks formed by Isola Bella, the rocks surrounding it and the stacks rising like Homeric giants in front of Capo Taormina. Here nature has the upper hand over everything. The sun beats down inexorably on the rocks, the rocky ravines, the shingly inlets and the mostly though and occasionally tempestuous waters of the Ionian Sea. In this magically seductive setting you can almost hear the song of the sirens, the legendary enchantresses of seamen or the modern temptresses of those who need to escape from the humdrum routine of daily life. The fish-laden waters of the bay are an irresistible invitation to scuba-divers, just as the Aeolian breezes are an inspiration for surfers and sailers. Lazier visitors can always bask under the Sicilian sun, either in secluded inlets along the coast or on the quiet beaches of the bay. At Capo Taormina a modern hotel equipped with swimming pools and every comfort offers the necessary quiet to tourists and conference parties alike.

Baia delle Sirene, a delightful view of the romantic inlet with Isola Bella; a detail of Isola Bella with the stacks of Capo Taormina in the background.

Baia delle Sirene, an aerial view of Isola Bella; a detail of the sandy shore.

ISOLA BELLA

Isola Bella is little more than a large rock in the centre of the enchanting Baia delle Sirene, just in front of the point where the two crescent-shaped bays meet. The island is cloaked in typical Mediterranean macchia, enriched by the presence of palms and cypresses. At its highest point a house stands like a dream home for the lucky few, or the memory of a dwelling just like any other, perhaps one that is no longer used. Numerous rocks encircle the island, luring swimmers, and offering a refuge for the numerous varieties of fish which inhabit this extraordinarily crystal-clear sea. From this secluded corner of the Ionian coast we can gaze along the enchanting coast and beyond the Strait towards the coasts of Calabria, dominated by the towering peaks of Aspromonte.

CAPO SANT'ANDREA

Situated at the far end of the Baia delle Sirene, Capo Sant'Andrea is an inseparable part of the picturesque Taormina seascape. The outline of its coast is jagged, with many ravines and natural coves. These are a true paradise for scuba-divers, but they also attract nature-lovers who can make pleasant boat excursions and explore the dream-like inlets of this intensely Mediterranean stretch of coast.

GROTTA AZZURRA

The largest of a series of natural cavities along the coast of Capo Sant'Andrea, this grotto certainly does not overshadow its far better-known namesake on the island of Capri. On the other hand it is not the only one on the Italian coast to bear the same name as the most famous grotto in the world. Boat excursions, which can be made from the Baia delle Sirene and from Mazzarò, make it possible to explore the fabulous grotto, where the reflections of light on the waters of the sea generate magical effects and intense plays of colour.

Baia delle Sirene, panoramic view towards Isola Bella and Capo Sant'Andrea; a suggestive image of Capo Taormina and its stacks.

Capo Taormina, a view of the stacks emerging from the transparent blue waters of the Ionian Sea; Capo Sant'Andrea, the entrance to the fabulous Grotta Azzurra, a popular tourist attraction.

Lido di Mazzarò, these photographs show some colourful aspects of this charming seaside resort.

Lido di Mazzarò, panoramic view of the marina and the hotel centre.

On the following page: Lido di Mazzarò, two images reflecting the tranquillity of this peaceful seaside resort.

LIDO DI MAZZARÒ

A famous holiday and seaside resort, Lido di Mazzarò grew up from an old fishing village. It overlooks a charming crescent-shaped bay, set off by the shimmering blue of the Ionian Sea, which is darker or lighter depending on the depth of the water and the slant of the sun's rays. Officially, Mazzarò is a coastal hamlet in the commune of Taormina. There is a continuity of Mediterranean atmospheres, of Ionian enchantment and Sicilian fragrances, the same continuity linking the small, fashionable seaside resort with the haughty and somewhat detached hilltop town of Taormina, rich as it is in archeological, monumental and cultural treasures. Together with other places nearby, however, it certainly contributes to that magical glamour and charm which is so admired by the numerous crowd of Italian and foreign visitors. After all a physical link also exists between Taormina and one of its main beaches. Tourists have only the embarrassment of the choice to get from Taormina to the sea and back. They can go by car along *Via Pirandello* and then take the main road (SS. 144), or otherwise be tempted by the thrill of a ride on the time-saving scenic cableway, which runs from Via Pirandello to the centre of the sea-side resort. Walkers, trained hikers or just simple lovers of healthy exercise can practise their favourite recreational activity on the idyllic slopes of the Taormina hillside, accompanied by inevitable sunshine, clear, deep-blue skies, the scent of jasmine and orange blossom and the salty air breezing in off the sea. For them we would recommend the pedestrian route, a series of steps departing from the scenic observation point situated on a hairpin bend of the *Via Pirandello*. Lido di Mazzarò looks like an evergreen garden, immersed as it is in the midst of numerous gardens, parks overflowing with the luxuriant vegetation of the Mediterranean macchia, agave, palm trees, cypresses, olives and cacti. The latter are evidence of an exceptional climate, beneficent for human beings throughout the year. This is the excuse for, and the substance of, a leisurely or recreational sojourn in Mazzarò, with the atmosphere of the past, yet with the comforts of the present within easy reach. A liberal smattering of hotels (all classes), many in idyllic settings and with every convenience, a tidy and well-equipped beach, numerous locales and entertainment, complete the picture of a place enjoying increasing popularity among tourists.

On the previous page: Giardini-Naxos, the suggestive view of snow-capped Etna is a wonderful natural backdrop to the Ionian seascape.

Giardini, a fine view of the bay.

Giardini: Castelmola, Taormina and Monte Tauro frame the broad fringe of the sandy shore; Naxos, the Bourbon Fort housing the Archeological Museum.

GIARDINI - NAXOS

The name Giardini-Naxos commonly indicates that stretch of densely populated coast situated in the centre of the enchanting bay of the same name. It is in fact a clear example of bipolar settlement: the first human settlements rose and developed around Capo Schisò (Naxos), while further north, in the industrial period and as a result of the great expansion of tourism (linked also to the fortunes of nearby Taormina), the more recent settlement of Giardini grew up. During the prehistoric age, a violent eruption of the volcano of Moio Alcàntara (present-day Monte Moio, 703m, the outermost of the temporary cones in the volcanic complex of Mount Etna), caused lava to flow along the natural conduit of the Alcàntara valley as far as the sea, thus forming what is now called Capo Schisò. Other sources suggest that the origin of the lavas of which this promontory is formed came from Etna itself. In 734 BC colonists from Chalcis, attracted by the beauty and by the natural fertility of the volcanic terrain, founded the colony of *Naxos* and raised an altar to Apollo Archegetes, venerated by the Hellenic colonists. In 403 BC the colony was destroyed by Dionysius I of Syracuse. The survivors took refuge on Monte Tauro and founded *Tauromenion*. A **Monument** at Giardini is evidence of another historic episode linked to the Italian Risorgimento. On 18 August 1860 Giuseppe Garibaldi, at the head of his legendary expeditionary corps, set off for Calabria from here in two steamboats.

Extensive remains of the **Walls**, dating from the 6th century BC, some **Gates** and a **Tower**, as well as the space that must have been occupied by a large **Sanctuary** survive from the old settlement of Naxos. In this immense area an ancient **Temple**, probably consecrated to the cult of *Aphrodite* (7th-5th century BC), has been identified. An **Altar** and two **Kilns**, probably linked to the sanctuary, have also been found in the area. Another part of the archeological zone is occupied by the remains of the city, which was rebuilt following its destruction in 403 BC. Here, the remains of cult monuments and the workshops of vase-makers and statue modellers have been unearthed. Numerous finds discovered in the area (ceramics, clay material, sculptures, terracottas, fragments of architecture) are displayed in the **Museo Archeologico of Naxos**, which is housed in the old Bourbon fort on Capo Schisò. The charming town of Giardini, with its little fishing harbour and landing stages for pleasure craft, is a celebrated holiday resort. The long beach, which slopes gently down to the sea, and modern recreational infrastructures make it just one of the many touristic jewels along this enchanting stretch of the Ionian coast.

*Giardini, various aspects of the fishing
centre of the seaside resort.*

*Folklore in Taormina: the Sicilian cart, with its
richly painted decorations and ornaments, of
which a detail can be seen in the photograph, is a
symbolic representation of the island's history, a
genuine, honest expression of its popular culture.*

Capo Sant'Alessio, suggestive images of the fortified dolomitic promontory towering above the Ionian Sea.

CAPO SANT'ALESSIO

For those travelling along the Ionian coast road (SS. 144) in the direction of Messina, Capo Sant'Alessio appears as a beautifully unspoilt white dolomitic bastion towering above the sea. It is the same beauty, the same magic awe which inspired the Greeks to call it the 'Silvery Cape' (*Argennon Akron*). Characteristic of this promontory, whose precipitous cliffs plunge sheer into the deep-blue waters of the Ionian Sea, is the intensely evocative atmosphere created by the sound of the waves breaking on the rocks and bare cliffs accompanied by the shrill cries of the seagulls.

The cape is a natural fortification, and in the first half of the 14th century a **Castle** was built on it which still stands with its polygonal ground-plan and its imposing defense walls. A system of walls runs along the saddle of the cape, linking the old castle to a **Fort** consisting of two cylindrical structures one on top of the other, completely restructured by the British in the 19th century.

FORZA D'AGRÒ

This picturesque village, which has the typical characteristics of a medieval settlement, stands in a scenic position 420m above sea level. It can be reached by turning off the coast road at Capo Sant'Alessio and following a winding road which offers superb views of the Ionian Sea, the Strait of Messina and the nearby Calabrian coast. In records of the first half of the 12th century it appears that the hamlet *Vicum Agrillae* was donated to the Monastery of Santi Pietro e Paolo d'Agrò. Around the first half of the 14th century, new feudal owners fortified the ancient hamlet, beginning its revival and consequent expansion, revealed by the auspicious addition of the word 'Forza' in the name. The attraction of Forza d'Agrò in our times is a late 15th-century **Arch** with peculiar traces of Catalan Gothic. It stands on the steps leading to the **Chiesa della Triade**. Other noteworthy sights are the **Chiesa Madre della SS. Annunziata** (16th C. with Baroque additions) and the old **Castle**, strangely used as a cemetery.

Forza d'Agrò, the steps of the Chiesa della Triade, with its Catalan-Gothic Arch and the Baroque facade of the Chiesa Madre.

Forza d'Agrò, a detail of the Arch leading to the Church of the Triad.

The Alcàntara gorge from above and a close-up view of the crystalline waters of the Alcàntara river.

THE ALCÀNTARA GORGE

The Alcàntara gorge, an absolute must for tourists visiting the area, can be reached from Taormina-Giardini Naxos by following the main road inland (185) towards Francavilla di Sicilia for 13 kilometres. This natural monument of basalt rock was created by the eruption of the *volcano Monte Moio*, Etna's most eccentric offshoot, around the year 2400 BC. The lava flow invaded the entire valley of the Alcàntara river as far as its mouth on the coast, where the Greeks founded their first colony in Sicily.

In the Sciara Lardcria region the river of lava reached a thickness of 70 metres. While still white-hot, and due to a telluric settling, a sinuous longitudinal crack opened in the lava over a length of 500 metres, 70 metres deep and five metres wide, thus assuming the structure of a gorge. Only later, all the waters of the catchment basin feeding the Alcàntara river flowed into the fissure and from this derived the name "Alcàntara gorge". The continuous action of the water smoothed the basalt walls of the gorge producing that gleaming lustre which can be admired only under the action of light.

The gorge is reached by way of a scenic footpath or by means of modern elevators. To reach the entrance of the gorge the use of wading boots is recommended, which can be hired at the site; these are a useful protection against the icy water and spiky rocks. The gorge is always a dangerous place for non-experts and those who are unfamiliar with the site.

There is a large car-park, a bar, a restaurant and farm holiday facilities; it is possible to stay the night, and taste and buy excellent food prepared with traditional recipes.

MOUNT ETNA

The volcanic structure of Mount Etna grew out of the depths of an extensive marine gulf which in the Quaternary Period submerged the present-day plain of Catania. The Etna area lies between the depressions of the Alcàntara valley in the north and the Simeto valley in the west and south. The fascinating landscape of Etna, in which the work of man, both at the level of cultivation and of fixed settlements (perennially threatened by the implacable activity of the volcano), is characterized by its multi-faceted nature. The many aspects of human activity are clearly conditioned by altitude zones. Up to 500m above sea level Etna's piedmont area is characterized by natural springs, by the high concentration of human settlement and by the dense cultivation of citrus fruit orchards. Higher up the human settlements thin out, giving way to the cultivation of vines and to the Mediterranean macchia, which reaches even up to 1300m. This is also the altitude belt of woodland, composed of various tree species (chestnut, birch, beech, larch, holm oak, pine and oak). In the zone between 1000 and 2000m there are numerous subsidiary cones (about 200 groups), situated along the slopes and at the base of the central crater. This is the area of the most intense volcanic activity. At 2000m shrubs, cryptogamic flora and scattered pastures replace the trees. Towards 2900m the volcanic activity is less intense. There is an extensive plateau, harsh and barren, where the terminal crater rises from the centre of a truncated cone. Towards the Ionian Sea is the awesome cleft called the Valle del Bove, one of the natural routes preferred by the magma which pours from the erupting craters. The *Colonna del Cielo*, as Pindar described it, was called *Aitnè* by the Greeks (probably from a verb meaning 'to flame' or 'to burn'), *Aetna* by the Romans, *Gebel* by the Arabs (or 'La Montagna', the term by which it is still known in popular usage, or more elegantly, *Mongibello*).

Etna is the largest volcano in Europe. Like all active volcanoes, however, its height is subject to variation, presently being fixèd at 3350m. The mountain has a surface area of 1570 km^2 and its perimeter is almost 200km long. Because of its exceptional naturalistic, anthropic and environmental importance, the Etna area has been designated a national park, with the appropriate legal provisions of the Regione Sicilia. The many interesting excursions in the area make it an outstanding attraction for visitors to the island interested in seeing in person the spectacular manifestations of the volcano's almost continuous activity, with its peaks of rare and astonishing intensity. The highest part of the volcano has been exploited for snow sports, and suitable structures for the practice of the most varied winter discplines have been erected.

The remarkable volcanic complex of Mount Etna, which dominates the north-eastern part of the island, animated legends and myths from the earliest times. The many

Sunset on Mount Etna.

A spectacular image of the eruption of Etna.

eruptions occurring in the course of the centuries have contributed to altering the shape of the mountain, with the formation of new and subsidiary craters, and profoundly modifying the local orographic structure and its morphological composition. There have been 135 violent eruptions recorded in history; many more, of course, will have occurred before recorded history. The eruptions of 475 BC, 396 BC, 1329 and 1381 were among the most important recorded. In the last three, the magma flowed as far as the sea. One of the most disastrous eruptions was that of 1699, which caused the partial submersion of Catania, with lava flowing into the sea for almost a kilometre. Other eruptions were recorded in 1809, 1811, 1819, 1843, 1852, 1865, 1879, 1883, 1886, 1892 and 1899. The eruptions of the 20th century have been not only numerous, but often spectacular and prolonged; those of 1908, 1910, 1911, 1917, 1923 and 1928 were often marked by serious damage and destruction (Mascali). Other eruptions occurred in 1942, 1947 and 1949, while one of the volcano's longest eruptions took place between 1950 and 1951. Other eruptions, often on a large-scale, happened in 1957-58, 1971, 1974, 1979 and 1983.

On the latter occasion the practice of deviating the lava flow with explosives was experimented with the aim of protecting the inhabited settlements of the piedmont area threatened by the progress of the immense torrents of magma. This technique was again employed, with more satisfactory results, during the long and devastating eruption of 1992.

One of the most popular itineraries for a visit to the volcano leaves from Catania to **Nicolosi**, as far as the Cantoniera dell'Etna, from where it is possible to depart for a spectacular visit of the crater with the help of expert guides. Visitors should scrupulously heed the elementary rules of prudence and common sense, given the considerable danger of the terminal crater area due to the sometimes unpredictable emission of pyroclastic material. A particularly noteworthy excursion was a complete tour of the volcano using the Rifugio Sapienza as a base (1910m, destroyed in the eruption of 1992), with visits to interesting villages and the chance to admire one of the most typical and characteristic landscapes in Sicily. The same itinerary can now be covered by bus or by train, the 'Ferrovia Circumetnea'.

THE GEOLOGY OF MOUNT ETNA

Mount Etna is the largest volcano in Europe and one of the most important active volcanoes in the world. It towers 3,350 metres above sea-level and has an average diameter at the base of about 40 kilometres. The volcanic complex, most of it composed of numerous lava flows piled up one on top of the other, lies on a base of sedimentary rock. The first reliable information on the volcanic activity of Mount Etna is contained in the accounts of various writers who lived in pre-Christian times. Diodorus Siculus narrates the episode of the Sicanians who were forced to abandon the area surrounding the volcano due to an eruption, the episode dating from a period preceding the Trojan war, while Thucydides informs us that in the 5th century BC the area around Catania was invaded by a river of lava. The activity of the volcano actually began about 700,000 years ago, a long time before human beings learned to write. Initially the emission of volcanic material was not subaerial but took place on the sea bed, as proved by the existence of outcrops of "pillow lava". These are a series of irregular sphere-shaped masses which were produced by an accumulation of blocks of not yet consolidated volcanic material lying at the bottom of submarine slopes. The outer part of these "pillows", having cooled abruptly in contact with the sea water, formed a kind of vitreous crust which subsequently broke into pieces. The result is the present accumulation of breccia, called "hyaloclasts", in the spaces between the various blocks. Later, tectonic folding probably caused by the thrust of the magma, caused the emergence of the sea bed and consequently the start of the volcano's subaerial activity. Most of the materials produced by the volcano were formed of effusions of lava, which due to their considerable fluidity gave the volcanic complex a fairly smooth form, without harsh slopes, thus producing the classic morphology of a "shield volcano". Later the consistency of the magma changed, becoming more viscous, and explosive activity increased. This gave the volcano a more rugged appearance, with jagged slopes, typical of a volcanic complex composed of alternating deposits of lava flows and materials resulting from explosive activity. This type of volcanic complex is called a "composite volcano". By magma we mean molten silicate containing dissolved gases and crystals in suspension. A characteristic of magmas, and one that is fundamental in evaluating their explosiveness, is their "viscosity".

Viscosity is directly proportional to the acidity of the magma, that is, to the silica and alumina content, and inversely proportional to the temperature of the magma, as it also is to the presence of alkalis and iron and to the concentration of water and volatile elements. The greater the viscosity the more frequent the explosive phenomena of the magma are during the cooling phase, whereas in more fluid lavas the loss of gases is continuous and less violent. As a "composite volcano", Mount Etna has manifested alternating types of activity, both constructive and destructive, the latter being borne out by the extensive depressions called "calderas", one of the most obvious and important being the Valle del Bove. The activity of Mount Etna is prevalently effusive, with relatively tranquil emissions of lava whose speed rarely exceeds 15km/h, together with small explosions near the mouths where the emission of spectacular fountains of lava can be seen. This effusive character is mainly due to the fluidity of the magma, which is of a basaltic type, that is, relatively poor in silica and alumina and capable of reaching temperatures of almost 1200°C. Although most of Etna's activity is in the central zone, many eruptions take place on the slopes. These are generated by a system of radial fractures converging towards the centre along which numerous subsidiary cones have formed. Volcanoes are generally associated with areas of intense seismic activity, such as recently formed mountain chains, mid-ocean ridges or rift valleys, in which exceptional forces are unleashed due to complex interaction between lithospheric plates. Etna is in fact situated in an area of interaction between two of these plates: the African and European. Millions of years ago the result of these two plates pushing towards each other was the closing of the ancient ocean of Thethys. The collision of the African and European plates has been an extremely complex phenomenon, in a prevalently compressive regime there being local instances of pulling apart. The Etna area is in fact an example of this, the formation of the volcano itself being caused by such geological stretching. Because the lithosphere is rigid it has fractured, thus causing the magmas produced by the partial melting of the mantle (the part of planet lying beneath the earth's crust) to start rising. From a depth of about 20 kilometres, it is pushed up as far as the surface, where it has given and continues to give rise to eruptions of the volcano.

A view of the slopes of Mount Etna.

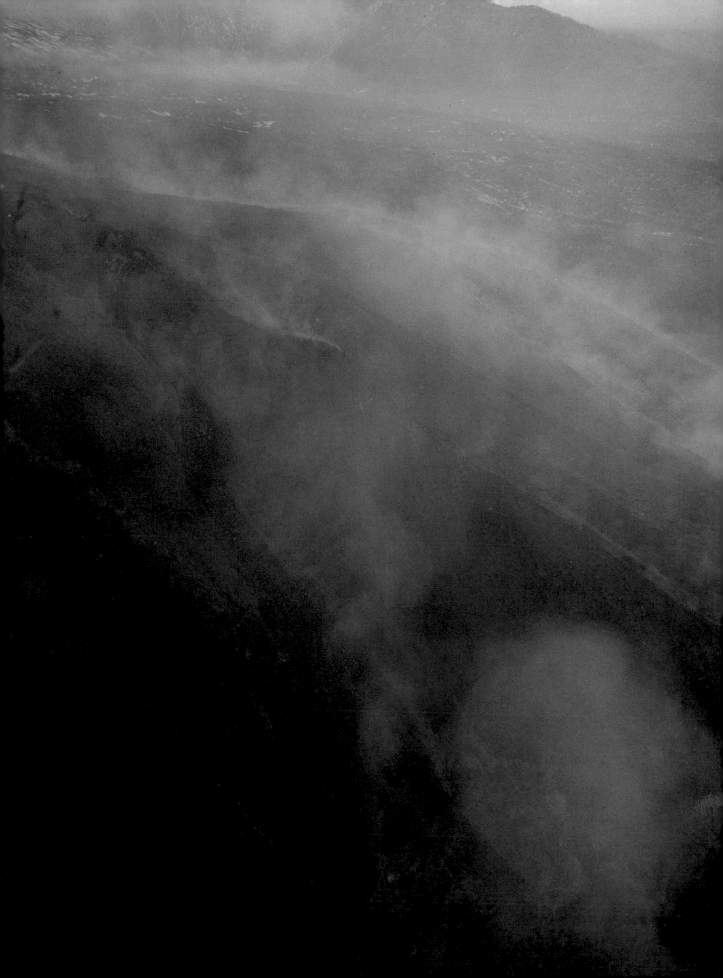